FAVORITE BRAND NAME™
BEST-LOVED RECIPES

Publications International, Ltd.

Favorite Brand Name Recipes at www.fbnr.com

Front cover photography by Proffitt Photography Ltd., Chicago

Pictured on the front cover *(clockwise from top right):* Chocolate Orange Marble Chiffon Cake *(page 260)*, Chicken Marsala *(page 196)*, Oven-Roasted Vegetables *(page 128)* and Insalata Rustica *(page 100)*.
Pictured on the back cover *(clockwise from top):* Orzotto with Herbs and Mushrooms *(page 128)*, Waldorf Salad with Turkey and Apricot *(page 92)*, Classic New York Cheesecake *(page 276)* and Veg•All® Italian Soup *(page 66)*.

Microwave Cooking: Microwave ovens vary in wattage. Use the cooking times as guidelines and check for doneness before adding more time.

Preparation/Cooking Times: Preparation times are based on the approximate amount of time required to assemble the recipe before cooking, baking, chilling or serving. These times include preparation steps such as measuring, chopping and mixing. The fact that some preparations and cooking can be done simultaneously is taken into account. Preparation of optional ingredients and serving suggestions is not included.

CONTENTS

❈ *Great Starters* ❈

Three Pepper Quesadillas

1 cup *each* thin green, red and yellow
    pepper strips
½ cup thin onion slices
½ teaspoon ground cumin
⅓ cup butter or margarine
1 package (8 ounces) PHILADELPHIA®
    Cream Cheese, softened

1 package (8 ounces) KRAFT® Shredded
    Sharp Cheddar Cheese
10 flour tortillas (6 inch)
    TACO BELL® HOME ORIGINALS®*
    Thick 'N Chunky Salsa

*TACO BELL and HOME ORIGINALS are registered trademarks owned and licensed by Taco Bell Corp.

COOK and stir peppers, onion and cumin in butter in large skillet 4 minutes or until vegetables are tender-crisp. Drain, reserving butter.

MIX cream cheese and Cheddar cheese until well blended. Spoon 2 tablespoons cheese mixture onto each tortilla; top with scant ⅓ cup vegetable mixture. Fold tortillas in half; place on cookie sheet. Brush with reserved butter.

BAKE at 425°F for 8 minutes. Cut each tortilla into thirds. Serve warm with salsa.

Makes 30 appetizers

Prep Time: 20 minutes
Bake Time: 8 minutes

Make-Ahead: Prepare as directed except for baking; cover. Refrigerate. When ready to serve, bake, uncovered, at 425°F, 15 to 18 minutes or until thoroughly heated.

Three Pepper Quesadillas

Hawaiian Ribs

1 can (8 ounces) crushed pineapple in juice, undrained
⅓ cup apricot jam
3 tablespoons *French's*® Classic Yellow® Mustard

1 tablespoon red wine vinegar
2 teaspoons grated peeled fresh ginger
1 clove garlic, minced
3 to 4 pounds pork baby back ribs*

*Or, if baby back ribs are not available, substitute 4 pounds pork spareribs, cut in half lengthwise. Cut spareribs into 3- to 4-rib portions. Cook 20 minutes in enough boiling water to cover. Grill ribs 30 to 40 minutes or until no longer pink near bone, brushing with portion of pineapple mixture during last 10 minutes.

1. Combine crushed pineapple with juice, apricot jam, mustard, vinegar, ginger and garlic in blender or food processor. Cover and process until very smooth.

2. Place ribs on oiled grid. Grill ribs over medium heat 40 minutes or until ribs are no longer pink near bone. Brush ribs with portion of pineapple sauce mixture during last 10 minutes of cooking. Cut into individual ribs to serve. Serve remaining sauce for dipping.

Makes 8 servings (1½ cups sauce)

Vegetable Hummus

2 cloves garlic
2 cans (15 to 19 ounces each) chick peas or garbanzo beans, rinsed and drained
1 package KNORR® Recipe Classics™ Vegetable Soup, Dip and Recipe Mix
½ cup water

½ cup olive oil
2 tablespoons lemon juice
¼ teaspoon ground cumin
6 (8-inch) whole wheat or white pita breads, cut into wedges

• In food processor, pulse garlic until finely chopped. Add remaining ingredients except pita bread. Process until smooth; chill at least 2 hours.

• Stir hummus before serving. If desired, add 1 to 2 tablespoons additional olive oil, or to taste. Serve with pita wedges.

Makes 3½ cups dip

Prep Time: 10 minutes
Chill Time: 2 hours

Hawaiian Ribs

Italian-Topped Garlic Bread

1 pound BOB EVANS® Italian Roll Sausage
1 (1-pound) loaf crusty Italian bread
½ cup butter, melted
2 teaspoons minced garlic

2 cups (8 ounces) shredded mozzarella cheese
2 cups diced tomatoes
8 ounces fresh mushrooms, sliced
3 tablespoons grated Parmesan cheese

Preheat oven to 325°F. Crumble and cook sausage in medium skillet until browned. Drain off any drippings. Cut bread into 1-inch slices. Combine butter and garlic in small bowl; brush bread slices with mixture. Arrange on ungreased baking sheet. Combine mozzarella cheese, tomatoes, mushrooms, Parmesan cheese and sausage; spread on bread slices. Bake 10 to 12 minutes or until cheese is melted and golden brown. Serve warm. Refrigerate leftovers.

Makes about 10 appetizer servings

Cheddar Cheese Puffs

Puffs
1 cup water
6 tablespoons butter, cut into pieces
1 teaspoon salt
   Pepper to taste
   Ground nutmeg (optional)
1 cup all-purpose flour
5 large eggs, divided

1 cup plus 3 tablespoons finely shredded Cheddar or Swiss cheese, divided

Filling
1 (11-ounce) jar NEWMAN'S OWN® All Natural Salsa
12 ounces cream cheese, softened

Preheat oven to 425°F. In heavy 2-quart saucepan, place water, butter, salt, pepper and nutmeg. When butter has melted and water is boiling, remove from heat. With wooden spoon, beat in flour all at once. (If mixture does not form a ball and leave the sides of pan clean, return to medium heat and beat vigorously for 1 to 2 minutes.) Remove from heat and beat in 4 eggs, 1 at a time, until each egg is thoroughly blended. Beat in 1 cup cheese. Place in pastry bag with ½-inch-diameter round tip and pipe 1-inch rounds on 2 greased baking sheets. Beat remaining egg. Brush tops of puffs with beaten egg and sprinkle with remaining cheese. Bake 20 to 25 minutes or until golden and crisp; turn off oven. Pierce each puff with a knife and return to cooling oven for 10 minutes to dry out. Remove and cool.

Drain approximately ¼ cup of liquid from salsa (reserve liquid for another use). Mix drained salsa with cream cheese and spoon filling into puffs.

Makes 36 appetizers

Italian-Topped Garlic Bread

Original Ranch® Spinach Dip

1 container (16 ounces) sour cream (2 cups)
1 box (10 ounces) frozen chopped spinach, thawed and squeezed dry
1 can (8 ounces) water chestnuts, rinsed, drained and chopped

1 packet (1 ounce) HIDDEN VALLEY® The Original Ranch® Salad Dressing & Seasoning Mix
1 loaf round French bread
Fresh vegetables, for dipping

Stir together sour cream, spinach, water chestnuts and salad dressing & seasoning mix. Chill 30 minutes. Just before serving, cut top off bread and remove center, reserving firm bread pieces. Fill bread bowl with dip. Cut reserved bread into cubes. Serve dip with bread and vegetables.

Makes 2½ cups dip

Humpty Dumpty's Favorite Chicken Nachos

4 boneless, skinless chicken breast halves (about 1¼ pounds)
2 tablespoons CRISCO® Oil*
1 packet (1¼ ounces) taco seasoning mix
2 cloves garlic, crushed
1 bag (10½ ounces) tortilla chips

1 can (16 ounces) refried beans
1 jar (16 ounces) prepared mild or medium chunky salsa
3 cups (1½ (8-ounce) packages) shredded Mexican pasteurized process cheese

Use your favorite Crisco Oil product.

Rinse chicken; pat dry. Cut into ¾-inch cubes. Combine oil, taco seasoning mix and garlic in medium bowl. Add chicken. Stir to coat.

Heat large nonstick skillet on medium heat. Add chicken, half at a time. Stir-fry about 5 minutes or until browned and no longer pink in center, reducing heat if necessary. Remove from skillet with slotted spoon.

Heat oven to 425°F.

Spread chips evenly in two 15×10-inch jelly roll pans. Sprinkle chicken over chips. Combine beans and salsa. Spoon over chicken and chips. Sprinkle with cheese.

Bake for 6 to 7 minutes or until cheese melts. Serve warm.

Makes 6 servings

Original Ranch® Spinach Dip

The Ultimate Onion

3 cups cornstarch
3½ cups all-purpose flour, divided
6 teaspoons paprika, divided
2 teaspoons garlic salt
1 teaspoon salt
1½ teaspoons black pepper, divided
2 bottles (24 ounces) beer

4 to 6 Colossal onions (4 inches in diameter)
2 teaspoons garlic powder
¾ teaspoon cayenne pepper, divided
1 pint mayonnaise (2 cups)
1 pint sour cream (2 cups)
½ cup chili sauce

1. For batter, mix cornstarch, 1½ cups flour, 2 teaspoons paprika, garlic salt, salt and 1 teaspoon black pepper in large bowl. Add beer; mix well. Set aside.

2. Cut about ¾-inch off top of each onion; peel onions. Being careful not to cut through bottom, cut onions into 12 to 16 wedges.

3. Soak cut onions in ice water for 10 to 15 minutes. If onions do not "bloom," cut petals slightly deeper. Meanwhile, prepare seasoned flour mixture. Combine remaining 2 cups flour, remaining 4 teaspoons paprika, garlic powder, remaining ½ teaspoon black pepper and ¼ teaspoon cayenne pepper in large bowl; mix well.

4. Dip cut onions into seasoned flour; remove excess by carefully shaking. Dip in batter; remove excess by carefully shaking. Separate "petals" to coat thoroughly with batter. (If batter begins to separate, mix thoroughly before using.)

5. Gently place onions, one at a time, in fryer basket and deep-fry at 375°F 1½ minutes. Turn onion over and fry 1 to 1½ minutes or until golden brown. Drain on paper towels. Place onion upright in shallow bowl and remove about 1 inch of "petals" from center of onion.

6. To prepare Creamy Chili Sauce, combine mayonnaise, sour cream, chili sauce and remaining ½ teaspoon cayenne pepper in large bowl; mix well. Serve warm onions with Creamy Chili Sauce.

Makes about 24 servings

Favorite recipe from **National Onion Association**

The Ultimate Onion

7-Layer Ranch Dip

1 envelope LIPTON® RECIPE SECRETS®
  Ranch Soup Mix
1 container (16 ounces) sour cream
1 cup shredded lettuce
1 medium tomato, chopped (about 1 cup)
1 can (2.25 ounces) sliced pitted ripe
  olives, drained

¼ cup chopped red onion
1 can (4.5 ounces) chopped green chilies,
  drained
1 cup shredded Cheddar cheese (about
  4 ounces)

1. In 2-quart shallow dish, combine soup mix and sour cream.

2. Evenly layer remaining ingredients, ending with cheese. Chill, if desired. Serve with tortilla chips.

Makes 7 cups dip

Prep Time: 15 minutes

Maple Baked Ribs

¼ cup I CAN'T BELIEVE IT'S NOT
  BUTTER!® Spread
2 cloves garlic, finely chopped
½ cup ketchup
⅓ cup pure maple syrup or pancake syrup

2 tablespoons firmly packed brown sugar
2 tablespoons white vinegar
2 teaspoons hot pepper sauce
2½ to 3 pounds baby back ribs or spareribs

Preheat oven to 400°F.

In small saucepan, melt I Can't Believe It's Not Butter! Spread over medium heat and cook garlic, stirring occasionally, 1 minute. Stir in ketchup, syrup, brown sugar, vinegar and hot pepper sauce. Bring to a boil over high heat. Reduce heat to low and simmer 2 minutes.

In bottom of broiler, without rack, arrange ribs. Pour maple sauce over ribs. Cover with aluminum foil and bake 45 minutes. Remove foil and bake an additional 10 minutes, basting once with sauce. With knife, slice between ribs and toss with sauce in bottom of pan.

Makes 4 servings

7-Layer Ranch Dip

Spicy Shrimp Cocktail

2 tablespoons olive or vegetable oil
¼ cup finely chopped onion
1 tablespoon chopped green bell pepper
1 clove garlic, minced
1 can (8 ounces) CONTADINA® Tomato Sauce

1 tablespoon chopped pitted green olives, drained
¼ teaspoon red pepper flakes
1 pound cooked shrimp, chilled

1. Heat oil in small skillet. Add onion, bell pepper and garlic; sauté until vegetables are tender. Stir in tomato sauce, olives and red pepper flakes.

2. Bring to a boil; simmer, uncovered, for 5 minutes. Cover.

3. Chill thoroughly. Combine sauce with shrimp in small bowl.

Makes 6 servings

Molded Seafood Mousse

¾ cup boiling water
1 package (4-serving size) JELL-O® Brand Lemon Flavor Gelatin Dessert
¼ teaspoon salt
1 cup BREAKSTONE'S® Sour Cream
½ cup KRAFT® Mayo: Real Mayonnaise or MIRACLE WHIP® Salad Dressing

2 tablespoons horseradish
2 tablespoons lemon juice
2 tablespoons grated onion
2 cups seafood*
1½ teaspoons dill weed

Suggested Seafood:1 can (15 or 16 ounces) red salmon, drained and flaked, 2 cans (6 ounces each) crabmeat, drained and flaked, 2 cups chopped cooked shrimp, 2 cups chopped imitation crabmeat.

STIR boiling water into gelatin and salt in large bowl at least 2 minutes until completely dissolved. Stir in sour cream, mayonnaise, horseradish, lemon juice and onion. Refrigerate about 1½ hours or until thickened (spoon drawn through leaves definite impression). Stir in seafood and dill weed. Spoon into 4-cup mold.

REFRIGERATE 3 hours or until firm. Unmold. Serve as an appetizer with crackers and raw vegetables.

Makes 12 servings

Spicy Shrimp Cocktail

Sweet Pepper Pizza Fingers

2 tablespoons margarine or butter
2 large red, green and/or yellow bell
   peppers, thinly sliced
1 clove garlic, finely chopped
1 envelope LIPTON® RECIPE SECRETS®
   Onion Soup Mix

1 cup water
1 package (10 ounces) refrigerated pizza
   crust
1½ cups shredded mozzarella cheese (about
   6 ounces)

Preheat oven to 425°F.

In 12-inch skillet, melt margarine over medium heat; cook peppers and garlic, stirring occasionally, 5 minutes or until peppers are tender. Stir in soup mix blended with water. Bring to a boil over high heat. Reduce heat to low and simmer uncovered 6 minutes or until liquid is absorbed. Remove from heat; set aside to cool 5 minutes.

Meanwhile, on large baking sheet sprayed with nonstick cooking spray, roll out pizza crust into 12×8-inch rectangle. Sprinkle 1 cup mozzarella cheese over crust; top with cooked pepper mixture, spreading to edges of dough. Top with remaining ½ cup mozzarella cheese. Bake 10 minutes or until crust is golden brown and topping is bubbly. Remove from oven and let stand 5 minutes. To serve, cut into 4×1-inch strips. *Makes about 24 appetizers*

Tip: Serve as a main dish by cutting pizza into Sicilian-style square pieces.

Pineapple-Almond Cheese Spread

2 cans (8 ounces each) DOLE® Crushed
   Pineapple
1 package (8 ounces) cream cheese,
   softened
4 cups (16 ounces) shredded sharp
   Cheddar cheese
½ cup mayonnaise

1 tablespoon soy sauce
1 cup chopped natural almonds, toasted
½ cup finely chopped DOLE® Green Bell
   Pepper
¼ cup minced green onions or chives
   DOLE® Celery stalks or assorted breads

• Drain pineapple. In large bowl, beat cream cheese until smooth; beat in Cheddar cheese, mayonnaise and soy sauce until smooth. Stir in pineapple, almonds, green pepper and onions. Refrigerate, covered. Use to stuff celery stalks or serve as spread with assorted breads. Serve at room temperature. *Makes 4 cups spread*

Sweet Pepper Pizza Fingers

Skewered Antipasto

1 jar (8 ounces) SONOMA® marinated
   dried tomatoes
1 pound (3 medium) new potatoes,
   cooked until tender
1 cup drained cooked egg tortellini and/or
   spinach tortellini
1 tablespoon chopped fresh chives *or*
   1 teaspoon dried chives

1 tablespoon chopped fresh rosemary *or*
   1 teaspoon dried rosemary
2 cups bite-sized vegetable pieces (such as
   celery, bell peppers, radishes, carrots,
   cucumber, green onions)

Drain oil from tomatoes into medium bowl. Place tomatoes in small bowl; set aside. Cut potatoes into 1-inch cubes. Add potatoes, tortellini, chives and rosemary to oil in medium bowl. Stir to coat with oil; cover and marinate 1 hour at room temperature. To assemble, alternately thread tomatoes, potatoes, tortellini and vegetables onto 6-inch skewers.   *Makes 12 to 14 skewers*

Cheesy Quiche Bites

36 RITZ® Crackers, finely crushed (about
   1½ cups crumbs)
3 tablespoons margarine or butter, melted
2 cups KRAFT® Shredded Cheddar Cheese
   (8 ounces)
½ cup chopped roasted red peppers

4 eggs, beaten
¾ cup milk
½ cup GREY POUPON® Dijon or
   COUNTRY DIJON® Mustard
¼ cup chopped fresh parsley
¼ cup KRAFT® Grated Parmesan Cheese

1. Mix cracker crumbs and margarine or butter; press onto bottom of greased 13×9×2-inch pan. Bake at 350°F for 8 to 10 minutes or until golden. Remove from oven; let stand for 5 minutes.

2. Sprinkle half the Cheddar cheese over crust; top with peppers and remaining Cheddar cheese.

3. Blend eggs, milk, mustard and parsley in small bowl; pour evenly over cheese in prepared pan. Sprinkle with Parmesan cheese. Bake at 350°F for 30 to 35 minutes or until set. Let stand 10 minutes; cut into 2×1½-inch bars. Serve warm.   *Makes 32 appetizers*

Prep Time: 30 minutes
Bake Time: 38 minutes
Total Time: 1 hour and 8 minutes

Skewered Antipasto

Savory Bruschetta

¼ **cup olive oil**
1 clove garlic, minced
1 loaf (1 pound) French bread, cut in half lengthwise
1 package (8 ounces) PHILADELPHIA® Cream Cheese, softened

3 tablespoons KRAFT® 100% Grated Parmesan Cheese
2 tablespoons chopped pitted Niçoise olives
1 cup chopped plum tomatoes
Fresh basil leaves

MIX oil and garlic; spread on cut surfaces of bread. Bake at 400°F for 8 to 10 minutes or until toasted. Cool.

MIX cream cheese and Parmesan cheese with electric mixer on medium speed until blended. Stir in olives. Spread on cooled bread halves.

TOP with tomatoes and basil leaves. Cut into slices.   *Makes 2 dozen appetizers*

Prep Time: 15 minutes
Bake Time: 10 minutes

Quick Sausage Appetizers

½ **pound BOB EVANS® Italian Roll Sausage**
⅓ **cup mozzarella cheese**
¼ **cup sour cream**

3 tablespoons mayonnaise
2 tablespoons chopped green onion
½ **teaspoon Worcestershire sauce**
10 slices white bread*

*Party rye or thinly sliced French bread may be used instead of white bread. Double recipe to have enough sausage mixture.

Preheat broiler. Crumble and cook sausage in medium skillet until browned. Drain on paper towels. Transfer sausage to small bowl; stir in mozzarella cheese, sour cream, mayonnaise, green onion and Worcestershire sauce. Cut crusts from bread. Cut each bread slice into 4 squares; spread about 1 teaspoon sausage mixture onto each square. Arrange squares on ungreased baking sheet; place under hot broiler just until cheese melts and topping bubbles. (Be careful not to burn corners and edges.) Serve hot.   *Makes 40 appetizer squares*

Note: Quick Sausage Appetizers may be made ahead and refrigerated overnight or frozen up to 1 month before broiling.

Savory Bruschetta

Buffalo Hot Wings

**24 TYSON® Individually Fresh Frozen®
Chicken Wings**
½ teaspoon salt
⅛ teaspoon black pepper

2 tablespoons butter
2 tablespoons hot sauce
½ teaspoon white vinegar

PREP: Preheat oven to 450°F. Line 15×11×1-inch baking pan with foil; spray with nonstick cooking spray. CLEAN: Wash hands. Arrange chicken in single layer on prepared pan. Sprinkle with salt and pepper. CLEAN: Wash hands.

COOK: Bake chicken 30 to 40 minutes or until internal juices of chicken run clear. (Or insert instant-read meat thermometer in thickest part of chicken. Temperature should read 170°F.) Meanwhile, in small saucepan, melt butter over medium heat. Add hot sauce and vinegar. Spread sauce over cooked chicken.

SERVE: Serve chicken with blue cheese dressing.

CHILL: Refrigerate leftovers immediately.

Makes 6 servings

Prep Time: 5 minutes
Cook Time: 40 minutes

Cheese Fondue

1½ cups dry white wine
**8 ounces (2 cups) Gruyère *or* Swiss cheese,
shredded**
2 tablespoons flour

**1 teaspoon TABASCO® brand Pepper
Sauce**
⅛ teaspoon salt
French bread cubes

Heat wine in 2-quart saucepan over low heat until boiling. Meanwhile, toss cheese with flour in medium bowl until blended.

Gradually add the cheese mixture to saucepan, stirring constantly until cheese melts. Stir in TABASCO® Sauce and salt. Serve immediately with French bread cubes for dipping.

Makes 2 servings

Hearty Fondue: Substitute 4 teaspoons TABASCO® New Orleans Style Steak Sauce for TABASCO® brand Pepper Sauce.

Ham-Chive Fondue: Stir ⅓ cup diced cooked ham and 1 tablespoon snipped chives into melted cheese mixture.

Spinach-Artichoke Cheese Squares

1 box (11 ounces) pie crust mix
1 container (15 ounces) part-skim ricotta cheese
½ cup grated Parmesan cheese
4 eggs
¼ cup plain dry bread crumbs
¼ cup *French's*® Napa Valley Style Dijon Mustard

1 teaspoon dried Italian seasoning
2 packages (10 ounces each) frozen chopped spinach, thawed and squeezed dry
1 jar (12 ounces) marinated artichoke hearts, drained and chopped
4 green onions, thinly sliced
½ cup chopped pimiento, well drained

1. Preheat oven to 400°F. Coat 15×10×1-inch baking pan with nonstick cooking spray. Toss pie crust mix with ⅓ cup cold water in large bowl until moistened and crumbly. Press mixture firmly onto bottom of prepared pan using floured bottom of measuring cup. Prick with fork. Bake 20 minutes or until golden.

2. Combine cheeses, eggs, bread crumbs, mustard and Italian seasoning in large bowl until well blended. Stir in vegetables; mix well. Spoon over baked crust, spreading evenly.

3. Bake 20 minutes or until toothpick inserted into center comes out clean. Cool on wire rack 15 minutes. Cut into squares. Serve warm or at room temperature.   *Makes 24 servings*

Prep Time: 25 minutes
Bake Time: 40 minutes

Guacamole

2 avocados, mashed
¼ cup red salsa (mild or hot, according to taste)
3 tablespoons NEWMAN'S OWN® Salad Dressing

2 tablespoons lime or lemon juice
1 clove garlic, finely minced
Salt
Black pepper

Combine all ingredients and mix well. Chill for 1 to 2 hours tightly covered. Serve with tortilla chips.
                                      Makes about 2 cups guacamole

Snappy Shrimp Zingers

2 cups finely chopped cooked, shelled shrimp
½ cup all-purpose flour
3 tablespoons finely chopped green onions
3 tablespoons finely chopped red bell pepper
1 tablespoon minced fresh parsley
1 tablespoon fresh lemon juice

2¼ teaspoons GEBHARDT® Hot Pepper Sauce
2 teaspoons Cajun seasoning
½ teaspoon salt
1 egg, slightly beaten
1 cup fine dry bread crumbs
2 cups WESSON® Canola Oil

In medium bowl, combine *first 9* ingredients, ending with salt; blend well. Add egg and blend until thoroughly combined. (Mixture will be sticky.) Shape mixture into 12 (3×¾-inch) stick-shaped pieces. Gently roll *each* piece in bread crumbs. In a large skillet, heat oil to 325°F. Gently place shrimp sticks into oil and fry until crisp and golden brown. Drain on paper towels. Serve with your favorite dipping sauce or a squeeze of lemon. *Makes about 12 zingers*

Ritz® Stuffed Mushrooms

20 medium mushrooms
2 tablespoons finely chopped onion
2 tablespoons finely chopped red bell pepper

3 tablespoons margarine or butter
14 RITZ® Crackers, finely crushed (about ½ cup crumbs)
½ teaspoon dried basil leaves

1. Remove stems from mushrooms; finely chop ¼ cup stems.

2. Cook and stir chopped stems, onion and bell pepper in margarine or butter in skillet over medium heat until tender. Stir in crumbs and basil.

3. Spoon crumb mixture into mushroom caps; place on baking sheet. Bake at 400°F for 15 minutes or until hot. *Makes 20 appetizers*

Prep Time: 20 minutes
Cook Time: 15 minutes
Total Time: 35 minutes

Snappy Shrimp Zingers

Party Chicken Sandwiches

1½ cups finely chopped cooked chicken
1 cup MIRACLE WHIP® or MIRACLE WHIP LIGHT Dressing
1 can (4 ounces) chopped green chilies, drained

¾ cup KRAFT® Shredded Sharp Cheddar Cheese
¼ cup finely chopped onion
36 party rye or pumpernickel bread slices

HEAT broiler.

MIX chicken, dressing, chilies, cheese and onion. Spread evenly onto bread slices.

BROIL 5 minutes or until lightly browned. Serve hot.   *Makes 3 dozen sandwiches*

Prep Time: 10 minutes
Broil Time: 5 minutes

Make-ahead: Prepare chicken mixture as directed; cover. Refrigerate. When ready to serve, spread bread with chicken mixture. Broil as directed.

Savory Cheese Ball

1 package (8 ounces) PHILADELPHIA® Cream Cheese, softened
1 package (8 ounces) KRAFT® Shredded Sharp Cheddar Cheese
¾ cup crumbled KRAFT® Natural Blue Cheese Crumbles

¼ cup chopped green onions
2 tablespoons milk
1 teaspoon Worcestershire sauce
PLANTERS® Finely Chopped Walnuts, Pecans, Cashews or Almonds

MIX cheeses, green onions, milk and Worcestershire sauce until well blended; cover. Refrigerate 1 to 2 hours.

SHAPE into ball; roll in nuts. Serve with TRISCUIT® Crackers and apple or pear slices.

Makes 2⅔ cups spread

Prep Time: 5 minutes plus refrigerating

Great Substitutes: Substitute 1 package (4 ounces) ATHENOS® Traditional Crumbled Feta Cheese for blue cheese.

Party Chicken Sandwiches

Chili Chip Party Platter

1 pound ground beef
1 medium onion, chopped
1 package (1.48 ounces) LAWRY'S® Spices & Seasonings for Chili
1 can (6 ounces) tomato paste
1 cup water

1 bag (8 to 9 ounces) tortilla chips or corn chips
1½ cups (6 ounces) shredded cheddar cheese
1 can (2¼ ounces) sliced pitted black olives, drained
½ cup sliced green onions

In medium skillet, cook ground beef until browned and crumbly; drain fat. Add onion, Spices & Seasonings for Chili, tomato paste and water; mix well. Bring to a boil over medium-high heat; reduce heat to low and simmer, uncovered, 15 minutes, stirring occasionally. Serve over tortilla chips. Top with cheddar cheese, olives and green onions. *Makes 4 servings*

Serving Suggestion: Serve with a cool beverage and sliced melon.

Smoked Turkey Roll-Ups

2 packages (4 ounces each) herb-flavored soft spreadable cheese
4 flour (8-inch diameter) tortillas*
2 packages (6 ounces each) smoked turkey breast slices

2 green onions, minced
¼ cup roasted red peppers, drained and finely chopped

To keep flour tortillas soft while preparing turkey roll-ups, cover with a slightly damp cloth.

1. Spread one package of cheese evenly over tortillas. Layer turkey slices evenly over cheese, overlapping turkey slices slightly to cover each tortilla. Spread remaining package of cheese evenly over turkey slices. Sprinkle with green onions and red peppers.

2. Roll up each tortilla jelly-roll style. Place roll-ups, seam side down, in resealable plastic bag; refrigerate several hours or overnight.

3. To serve, cut each roll-up crosswise into ½-inch slices to form pinwheels. If desired, arrange pinwheels on serving plate and garnish with red pepper slices in center.

Makes 56 appetizer servings

*Favorite recipe from **National Turkey Federation***

Chili Chip Party Platter

Shrimp Toast

¾ pound medium-size raw shrimp, peeled, deveined and minced
3 green onions, minced
1 tablespoon chopped fresh cilantro
1 teaspoon minced fresh ginger root
1 teaspoon KIKKOMAN® Soy Sauce
1 teaspoon dry sherry

1 teaspoon Oriental sesame oil
½ teaspoon salt
1 tablespoon cornstarch
1 egg, slightly beaten
8 slices day-old white bread, edges trimmed
2 cups vegetable oil

Combine shrimp, green onions, cilantro, ginger, soy sauce, sherry, sesame oil and salt in medium bowl. Blend in cornstarch. Stir in egg; blend thoroughly. Cut each bread slice diagonally in half to form triangles. Spread shrimp mixture evenly over bread, spreading out to edges. Heat vegetable oil in wok or large skillet over medium-high heat to 360°F. (Oil is ready when bread cube dropped into oil rises to surface.) Add 2 or 3 triangles to hot oil, shrimp side down. Deep-fry about 30 seconds until edges begin to brown; turn over and deep-fry about 30 seconds longer, or until golden brown and crispy. Drain on paper towels, shrimp side down; keep warm. Repeat procedure with remaining triangles. To serve, cut each shrimp triangle diagonally in half. *Makes about 8 appetizer servings*

Sweet and Sour Meatballs

Meatballs
  ½ cup instant rice
  2 pounds lean ground beef
  1 egg
  1 cup soft butter-flavored cracker crumbs*
  2 tablespoons oil

Sauce
  1½ cups barbecue sauce
  1 cup (12-ounce jar) SMUCKER'S® Pineapple Topping
  ¼ cup firmly packed brown sugar

You may substitute croutons or stuffing mix for the crackers.

Prepare rice according to package directions.

Meanwhile, combine ground beef, egg and cracker crumbs; mix well. Add cooked rice; mix thoroughly. Shape into 1½- or 2-inch meatballs. Cook in oil over medium heat until browned, turning occasionally. If necessary, drain grease from skillet.

Combine all sauce ingredients; mix until brown sugar is dissolved. Pour over meatballs. Cover and simmer over low heat for 30 to 45 minutes or until meatballs are no longer pink in center. Serve with toothpicks. *Makes 4 to 6 servings*

Shrimp Toast

Deviled Eggs

12 large eggs, room temperature
1 tablespoon vinegar
Lettuce leaves

Filling
3 tablespoons *Frank's® RedHot®* Cayenne Pepper Sauce

2 tablespoons mayonnaise
2 tablespoons sour cream
½ cup minced celery
¼ cup minced red onion
¼ teaspoon garlic powder

1. Place eggs in a single layer in bottom of large saucepan; cover with water. Add vinegar to water. Bring to a full boil. Immediately remove from heat. Cover; let stand 15 minutes. Drain eggs and rinse with cold water. Set eggs in bowl of ice water; cool.

2. To peel eggs, tap against side of counter. Gently remove shells, holding eggs under running water. Slice eggs in half lengthwise; remove yolks to medium bowl. Arrange whites on lettuce-lined platter.

3. To make Filling, add *Frank's RedHot* Sauce, mayonnaise and sour cream to egg yolks in bowl. Mix until well blended and creamy. Stir in celery, onion and garlic powder; mix well. Spoon about 1 tablespoon filling into each egg white. Garnish with parsley, capers or caviar, if desired. Cover with plastic wrap; refrigerate 30 minutes before serving.   *Makes 12 servings (about 1½ cups filling)*

Tip: Filling may be piped into whites through large star-shaped pastry tip inserted into corner of plastic bag.

Piggy Wraps

1 package HILLSHIRE FARM® Lit'l Smokies

2 (8-ounce) cans refrigerated crescent roll dough, cut into small triangles

Preheat oven to 400°F.

Wrap individual Lit'l Smokies in dough triangles. Bake 5 minutes or until golden brown.
      Makes about 50 hors d'oeuvres

Note: Piggy Wraps may be frozen. To reheat in microwave, microwave at HIGH 1½ minutes or at MEDIUM-HIGH (70% power) 2 minutes. When reheated in microwave, dough will not be crisp.

Hot Artichoke Dip

1 envelope LIPTON® RECIPE SECRETS® Onion Soup Mix*	1 cup HELLMANN'S® or BEST FOODS® Mayonnaise
1 can (14 ounces) artichoke hearts, drained and chopped	1 container (8 ounces) sour cream
	1 cup shredded Swiss or mozzarella cheese

Also terrific with LIPTON® RECIPE SECRETS® Savory Herb with Garlic, Golden Onion, or Onion Mushroom Soup Mix.

1. Preheat oven to 350°F. In 1-quart casserole, combine all ingredients.

2. Bake uncovered 30 minutes or until heated through.

3. Serve with your favorite dippers.   *Makes 3 cups dip*

Prep Time: 5 minutes
Bake Time: 30 minutes

Cold Artichoke Dip: Omit Swiss cheese. Stir in, if desired, ¼ cup grated Parmesan cheese. Do not bake.

Recipe Tip: When serving hot dip for a party, try baking it in 2 smaller casseroles. When the first casserole is empty, replace it with the second one, fresh from the oven.

Chicken Wings Teriyaki

½ cup teriyaki sauce	½ teaspoon five spice powder
¼ cup HOLLAND HOUSE® Sherry Cooking Wine	¼ teaspoon sesame oil
2 tablespoons oil	2 cloves garlic, finely chopped
2 tablespoons honey	2 pounds chicken wings
1 teaspoon finely chopped peeled ginger	¼ cup sliced scallions
	1 tablespoon toasted sesame seeds

Heat oven to 375°F. In small bowl, combine teriyaki sauce, cooking wine, oil, honey, ginger, five spice powder, sesame oil and garlic. Pour into 13×9-inch pan. Add chicken wings, turning to coat all sides. Bake for 35 to 45 minutes or until chicken is tender and cooked through, turning once and basting occasionally with sauce.* Sprinkle with scallions and sesame seeds.   *Makes 24 appetizers*
Do not baste during last 5 minutes of cooking.

❦ *Traditional Breads* ❦

Apple Cinnamon Rolls

5 to 5½ cups all-purpose flour
½ cup sugar
2 envelopes FLEISCHMANN'S®
  RapidRise™ Yeast
1 teaspoon salt
½ cup water

½ cup milk
¼ cup butter or margarine
3 large eggs
  Apple Filling (recipe follows)
  Cinnamon-Sugar Topping (recipe
  follows)

In large bowl, combine 1 cup flour, sugar, undissolved yeast, and salt. Heat water, milk, and butter until very warm (120° to 130°F). Gradually add to dry ingredients. Beat 2 minutes at medium speed of electric mixer, scraping bowl occasionally. Add eggs and 1 cup flour; beat 2 minutes at high speed, scraping bowl occasionally. Stir in enough remaining flour to make soft dough. Knead on lightly floured surface until smooth and elastic, about 8 to 10 minutes. Cover; let rest 10 minutes.

Divide dough into 2 equal portions. Roll each portion into 12×8-inch rectangle. Spread Apple Filling evenly over dough. Beginning at long end of each, roll up tightly jelly-roll style. Pinch seams to seal. Cut each roll into 12 equal pieces. Place, cut sides up, in greased 9-inch round pans. Cover; let rise in warm, draft-free place until doubled in size, about 45 minutes. Sprinkle with Cinnamon-Sugar Topping.

Bake at 375°F for 25 to 30 minutes or until done. Remove from pans; serve warm.

Makes 24 rolls

Apple Filling: Combine 2 large cooking apples, chopped, 2 tablespoons all-purpose flour, ¾ cup sugar, and ¼ cup butter or margarine in medium saucepan; bring to a boil over medium high heat. Cook 3 minutes. Reduce heat to medium-low; cook 10 minutes, stirring constantly until thick. Stir in 1 teaspoon ground cinnamon and ½ teaspoon nutmeg. Cool completely.

Cinnamon-Sugar Topping: Combine ¾ cup sugar, 1 teaspoon ground cinnamon, and ½ teaspoon nutmeg. Stir until well-blended.

Apple Cinnamon Rolls

Onion Buckwheat Bread

1 pound diced white onions
3 tablespoons olive oil
4½ teaspoons yeast
1½ cups water, at 90°F
½ cup milk
6½ cups unbleached bread flour
½ cup buckwheat flour
5 teaspoons sea salt

1 tablespoon finely chopped fresh rosemary
3 ounces shredded Gouda or Cheddar cheese
Unbleached bread flour as needed for kneading
4 tablespoons poppy seeds or nigella seeds (onion seeds)

1. Sauté onions in olive oil over medium high heat until just browned, about 5 minutes. Set aside to cool.

2. Combine yeast with water; let sit 10 minutes until creamy.

3. Add milk to yeast mixture and stir to combine. Gradually add bread flour, buckwheat flour, salt, rosemary and onions. When mixture is well combined, add cheese and blend. The dough will be slightly sticky.

4. Knead dough about 10 minutes, until smooth and elastic. Add additional bread flour as needed if dough is too soft.

5. Lightly oil clean bowl. Place dough in bowl; cover and let rise until doubled in bulk, about 1½ to 2 hours.

6. Gently punch down dough and place on lightly floured surface. Cut dough in half and shape into round ball. Spritz top of each loaf with water, and press into poppy seeds or nigella seeds. Place on lightly floured sheet pan; cover and let rise until almost doubled in bulk, 45 minutes to 1 hour.

7. Preheat oven to 450°F. Slash top of loaves with razor and place in oven. Add steam for first 10 minutes. *Reduce heat to 400°F* and bake an additional 35 to 40 minutes. Cool loaves completely on rack.

Makes 2 (10-inch) round loaves

Favorite recipe from **National Onion Association**

Onion Buckwheat Bread

Focaccia

1 cup water
1 tablespoon olive oil, plus additional for
  brushing
1 teaspoon salt
1 tablespoon sugar
3 cups bread flour

2¼ teaspoons RED STAR® Active Dry Yeast
Suggested toppings: sun-dried tomatoes,
  grilled bell pepper slices, sautéed
  onion rings, fresh and dried herbs of
  any combination, grated hard cheese

Bread Machine Method

Place room temperature ingredients, except toppings, in pan in order listed. Select dough cycle. Check dough consistency after 5 minutes of kneading, making adjustments if necessary.

Hand-Held Mixer Method

Combine yeast, 1 cup flour, sugar and salt. Combine water and 1 tablespoon oil; heat mixture to 120° to 130°F. Combine dry mixture and liquid mixture in mixing bowl on low speed. Beat 2 to 3 minutes on medium speed. By hand, stir in enough remaining flour to make firm dough. Knead on floured surface 5 to 7 minutes or until smooth and elastic. Add additional flour, if necessary.

Stand Mixer Method

Combine yeast, 1 cup flour, sugar and salt. Combine water and 1 tablespoon oil; heat mixture to 120° to 130°F. Combine dry mixture and liquid mixture in mixing bowl with paddle or beaters 4 minutes on medium speed. Gradually add remaining flour and knead with dough hook 5 to 7 minutes or until smooth and elastic. Add additional flour, if necessary.

Food Processor Method

Combine yeast, 1 cup flour, sugar and salt. Combine water and 1 tablespoon oil. Put dry mixture in processing bowl with steel blade. While motor is running, add liquid mixture. Process until mixed. Continue processing, adding remaining flour until dough forms a ball. Add additional flour, if necessary.

Rising, Shaping, and Baking

Place dough in lightly oiled bowl and turn to grease top. Cover; let rise until dough tests ripe.* Turn dough onto lightly floured surface; punch down to remove air bubbles. On lightly floured surface, shape dough into a ball. Place on greased cookie sheet. Flatten to 14-inch circle. With knife, cut circle in dough about 1 inch from edge, cutting almost through to cookie sheet. Pierce center with fork. Cover; let rise about 15 minutes. Brush with oil and sprinkle with desired toppings. Bake in preheated 375°F oven 25 to 30 minutes or until golden brown. Remove from cookie sheet to cool. Serve warm or cold.   *Makes 1 (14-inch) loaf*

Place two fingers into the dough and them remove them. If the holes remain the dough is ripe and ready to punch down.

Focaccia

Tropical Carrot Bread

Bread

⅓ CRISCO® Stick or ⅓ cup CRISCO® all-vegetable shortening plus additional for greasing
¾ cup firmly packed brown sugar
4 egg whites, slightly beaten
2¼ cups all-purpose flour
1 tablespoon plus 2 teaspoons baking powder
¾ teaspoon ground cinnamon
¼ teaspoon ground ginger
¼ teaspoon salt (optional)
1¼ cups uncooked old-fashioned or quick oats
1 cup shredded carrots
1 can (8 ounces) crushed pineapple in unsweetened juice
½ cup raisins

Topping

2 tablespoons uncooked old-fashioned or quick oats

1. Heat oven to 350°F. Grease 9×5×3-inch loaf pan.

2. For bread, combine shortening and brown sugar in large bowl. Beat at medium speed of electric mixer or stir with fork until well blended. Stir in egg whites. Beat until fairly smooth.

3. Combine flour, baking powder, cinnamon, ginger and salt in medium bowl. Stir into egg mixture. Stir in oats. Add carrots and pineapple with juice. Stir until just blended. Stir in raisins. Spoon into loaf pan.

4. For topping, sprinkle oats over top.

5. Bake at 350°F for 70 to 80 minutes or until toothpick inserted in center comes out clean. Cool 10 minutes in pan on rack. Loosen from sides. Remove from pan. Cool completely on rack.

Makes 1 loaf (12 servings)

Kitchen Hint: A loaf of homemade bread makes a great gift—especially when it's given in a new loaf pan. Just add a wooden spoon and the recipe, wrap it all up in a festive towel and tie it with ribbon.

Tropical Carrot Bread

Top Choice White Bread

5½ to 6 cups all-purpose flour
3 tablespoons sugar
2 envelopes FLEISCHMANN'S®
    RapidRise™ Yeast

2 teaspoons salt
1½ cups water
½ cup milk
2 tablespoons butter or margarine

In large bowl, combine 2 cups flour, sugar, undissolved yeast, and salt. Heat water, milk, and butter until very warm (120° to 130°F); stir into dry ingredients. Beat 2 minutes at medium speed of electric mixer, scraping bowl occasionally. Stir in 1 cup flour; beat at high speed for 2 minutes, scraping bowl occasionally. Stir in enough remaining flour to make soft dough. Knead on lightly floured surface until smooth and elastic, about 8 to 10 minutes. Cover; let rest 10 minutes.

Divide dough in half. Roll each half into 12×7-inch rectangle. Beginning at short end of each rectangle, roll up tightly as for jelly roll. Pinch seams and ends to seal. Place seam sides down, in 2 greased 8½×4½-inch loaf pans. Cover; let rise in warm, draft-free place until doubled in size, about 45 minutes.

Bake at 400°F for 25 to 30 minutes or until done. Remove from pans; cool on wire rack.

Makes 2 loaves

Mallomar® Sticky Buns

1 (8-ounce) package refrigerated crescent
    roll dough
8 MALLOMARS® Chocolate Cakes

Powdered sugar glaze and melted
    semisweet chocolate, optional

1. Separate crescent roll dough into 8 triangles.

2. Wrap each dough triangle around one cake, pinching seams to seal. Place in 8-inch round cake pan.

3. Bake at 375°F for 15 to 17 minutes or until golden brown. Cool in pan on wire rack for 15 minutes. Remove from pan to serving plate; drizzle with powdered sugar glaze and melted chocolate if desired. Serve warm.

Makes 8 buns

Prep Time: 25 minutes
Cook Time: 15 minutes

Chocolate Chunk Cinnamon Coffee Cake

1 package (12 ounces) BAKER'S®
    Semi-Sweet Chocolate Chunks
¾ cup chopped nuts
2 cups sugar, divided
1½ teaspoons cinnamon
2⅔ cups flour
1½ teaspoons baking soda

¾ teaspoon CALUMET® Baking Powder
½ teaspoon salt
¾ cup (1½ sticks) butter, softened
1 teaspoon vanilla
3 eggs
1½ cups BREAKSTONE'S® or KNUDSEN®
    Sour Cream

HEAT oven to 350°F. Grease 13×9-inch baking pan.

MIX chocolate, nuts, ⅔ cup sugar and cinnamon; set aside. Mix flour, baking soda, baking powder and salt; set aside.

BEAT butter, remaining 1⅓ cups sugar and vanilla in large bowl with electric mixer on medium speed until light and fluffy. Add eggs, 1 at a time, beating well after each addition. Add flour mixture alternately with sour cream, beating after each addition until smooth. Spoon ½ of the batter into prepared pan. Top with ½ of the chocolate-nut mixture. Repeat layers.

BAKE 40 to 45 minutes or until toothpick inserted in center comes out clean. Cool in pan on wire rack. *Makes 16 servings*

Potato Dill Biscuits

1 medium COLORADO potato, peeled
    and chopped
½ cup water
2 cups all-purpose flour
1 tablespoon baking powder
2 teaspoons sugar

1 teaspoon dried dill weed
½ teaspoon cream of tartar
½ teaspoon salt
¼ cup shortening
¼ cup butter

In small saucepan combine chopped potato and ½ cup water. Cover and cook over medium heat about 10 minutes or until potato is tender. *Do not drain.* Mash until smooth. Add additional water to measure 1 cup. In mixing bowl combine flour, baking powder, sugar, dill, cream of tartar and salt. Cut in shortening and butter until mixture resembles coarse crumbs. Add potato mixture. Stir just until mixture clings together. On lightly floured surface, knead dough 10 or 12 times. Pat into 8-inch square. Cut into 16 squares. Place biscuits on baking sheet. Bake in 450°F oven 10 to 12 minutes or until lightly browned. Serve warm. *Makes 16 biscuits*

Favorite recipe from **Colorado Potato Administrative Committee**

Chocolate Chunk Cinnamon Coffee Cake

Hot Cross Buns

1 package (¼ ounce) active dry yeast
¼ cup warm water (105° to 115°F)
¾ cup warm milk
¼ cup GRANDMA'S® Molasses
4 tablespoons (½ stick) butter, softened
2 eggs
1½ teaspoons salt

3½ cups all-purpose flour, divided
1 teaspoon cinnamon
½ teaspoon nutmeg
¼ teaspoon allspice
½ cup currants or raisins
2 tablespoons chopped candied citron

1. In large bowl, stir yeast into water and let stand several minutes to dissolve. Combine milk, molasses, butter, eggs and salt in large bowl; beat well. Add yeast mixture; mix well. Beat in 1½ cups flour, cinnamon, nutmeg and allspice. Cover bowl and let rise about 1 hour or until bubbly or double in bulk.

2. Add remaining 2 cups flour and blend well, adding additional flour if necessary to make dough firm enough to handle. Turn onto floured surface; knead dough until firm and elastic. Add currants and citron during last 5 minutes of kneading. Place dough in greased bowl; cover and let rise until double in bulk.

3. Heat oven to 375°F. Punch dough down; turn onto lightly floured surface. Roll into 14×10-inch rectangle, about ½ inch thick. Cut dough with 2½- to 3-inch round cutter; place buns about 1 inch apart on greased baking sheets. Gather up scraps, reroll and continue cutting until all dough has been used. Let rise, uncovered, until double in bulk.

4. Just before baking, use floured scissors to snip cross in tip of each bun, cutting about ½ inch deep. Bake about 15 minutes or until tops of buns are golden brown. Remove from oven and transfer to rack to cool.

Makes 12 buns

Fred's Raspberry Cream Cheese Coffee Cake

2¼ cups all-purpose flour
1 cup sugar, divided
¾ cup butter or margarine, cut into 12 pieces
½ teaspoon baking powder
½ teaspoon baking soda
¼ teaspoon salt
¾ cup sour cream
2 eggs, divided

1 teaspoon almond extract
1 (8-ounce) package cream cheese, softened
½ teaspoon grated lemon peel
½ teaspoon vanilla
½ cup SMUCKER'S® Seedless Red Raspberry Jam
½ cup slivered almonds

Grease and flour bottom and side of 10-inch springform pan. In large bowl, combine flour and ¾ cup of the sugar. Using pastry blender, cut in butter until mixture resembles coarse crumbs. Reserve 1 cup crumb mixture.

To remaining crumb mixture, add baking powder, baking soda, salt, sour cream, 1 of the eggs and almond extract; blend well. Spread batter over bottom and 2 inches up side of prepared pan. Batter should be about ¼ inch thick on side.

Combine cream cheese, remaining ¼ cup sugar, remaining egg, lemon peel and vanilla; blend well. Spread over batter in pan. Spoon jam evenly over cream cheese filling.

Combine reserved crumb mixture and almonds. Sprinkle over top.

Bake at 350°F for 45 to 55 minutes or until cream cheese filling is set and crust is deep golden brown. Cool 15 minutes. Remove side of pan. Serve warm or cool. Refrigerate leftovers.

Makes 12 servings

Monkey Bread

½ pound butter, melted
2 teaspoons LAWRY'S® Garlic Powder with Parsley

4 packages (9.5 ounces each) refrigerated buttermilk biscuits

In medium bowl, combine butter and Garlic Powder with Parsley; mix well. Separate biscuits and dip each into butter to coat. In tube pan, place one layer of dipped biscuits in bottom, slightly overlapping each biscuit. Arrange remaining biscuits in zig-zag fashion, some towards center and some towards outside edge of pan. Use all biscuits in as many layers as needed. Pour half of remaining butter over biscuits. Bake, uncovered, in 375°F oven 15 to 20 minutes. Invert onto serving platter and pour remaining butter over bread. Serve warm. *Makes 10 to 12 servings*

Old-Fashioned Cake Doughnuts

3¾ cups all-purpose flour
1 tablespoon baking powder
1 teaspoon ground cinnamon
¾ teaspoon salt
½ teaspoon ground nutmeg
3 eggs
¾ cup granulated sugar

1 cup applesauce
2 tablespoons butter, melted
1 quart vegetable oil
2 cups sifted powdered sugar
3 tablespoons milk
½ teaspoon vanilla
Colored sprinkles (optional)

Combine flour, baking powder, cinnamon, salt and nutmeg in medium bowl. Beat eggs in large bowl with electric mixer at high speed until frothy. Gradually beat in granulated sugar. Continue beating at high speed 4 minutes until thick and lemon colored, scraping down side of bowl once. Reduce speed to low; beat in applesauce and butter.

Beat in flour mixture until well blended. Divide dough into halves. Place each half on large piece of plastic wrap. Pat each half into 5-inch square; wrap in plastic wrap. Refrigerate 3 hours or until well chilled.

Pour oil into large Dutch oven. Place deep-fry thermometer in oil. Heat oil over medium heat until thermometer registers 375°F. Adjust heat as necessary to maintain temperature at 375°F. To prepare glaze, stir together powdered sugar, milk and vanilla in small bowl until smooth. Cover; set aside. Roll out 1 dough half to ⅜-inch thickness. Cut dough with floured 3-inch doughnut cutter; repeat with remaining dough. Reserve doughnut holes. Reroll scraps; cut dough again.

Place 4 doughnuts and holes in hot oil. Cook 2 minutes or until golden brown, turning often. Remove with slotted spoon; drain on paper towels. Repeat with remaining doughnuts and holes. Spread glaze over warm doughnuts; decorate with sprinkles, if desired.

Makes 12 doughnuts and holes

Old-Fashioned Cake Doughnuts

Braided Sandwich Ring

Dough
¾ cup buttermilk, at 80°F
2 large eggs, at room temperature
2 tablespoons vegetable oil
3 tablespoons sugar
1½ teaspoons salt
4 cups bread flour
2¼ teaspoons RED STAR® Active Dry Yeast

Glaze
1 egg
1 tablespoon milk
1 tablespoon sesame or poppy seeds

Filling
Mayonnaise, lettuce, sliced tomatoes, onion rings, sliced olives, sliced deli meats, sliced cheeses, Dijon mustard

Bread Machine Method
Place dough ingredients in pan in order listed. Select dough cycle. Check dough consistency after 5 minutes of kneading making adjustments if necessary.

Hand-Held Mixer Method
Combine 1 cup flour, sugar, yeast and salt. Heat buttermilk to 120° to 130°F. Combine flour mixture, buttermilk, 2 eggs and oil in mixing bowl on low speed. Beat 2 to 3 minutes on medium speed. By hand, stir in enough remaining flour to make firm dough. Knead on floured surface 5 to 7 minutes or until smooth and elastic. Use additional flour, if necessary. Place dough in lightly oiled bowl and turn to grease top. Cover; let rise until dough tests ripe.*

Stand Mixer Method
Combine 1 cup flour, sugar, yeast and salt. Heat buttermilk to 120° to 130°F. Combine flour mixture, buttermilk, 2 eggs and oil in mixing bowl with paddle or beaters 4 minutes on medium speed. Gradually add remaining flour and knead with dough hook 5 to 7 minutes or until smooth and elastic. Use additional flour, if necessary. Place dough in lightly oiled bowl and turn to grease top. Cover; let rise until dough tests ripe.*

Shaping and Baking
Punch down dough. Divide into three parts. On lightly floured surface, roll each third into 24-inch rope. On greased cookie sheet lightly sprinkled with cornmeal, loosely braid ropes from center to ends. Shape into circle; fasten ends by pinching dough together. Cover; let rise until indentation remains after touching.

For glaze, combine remaining 1 egg and milk; gently brush risen dough. Sprinkle with sesame seeds. Bake in preheated 375°F oven 25 to 35 minutes or until golden brown; cool.

Using serrated knife, slice ring crosswise to create large sandwich. Spread bottom half with mayonnaise; arrange filling ingredients on top of mayonnaise. Spread top section with mustard; place on top of filling. Slice into serving portions.   *Makes 1 sandwich ring*

*Place two fingers into the dough and then remove them. If the holes remain the dough is ripe and ready to punch down.

Braided Sandwich Ring

English-Style Scones

3 eggs, divided
½ cup heavy cream
1½ teaspoons vanilla
2 cups all-purpose flour
2 teaspoons baking powder
¼ teaspoon salt
¼ cup cold butter

¼ cup finely chopped pitted dates
¼ cup golden raisins or currants
1 teaspoon water
6 tablespoons no-sugar-added orange
    marmalade fruit spread
6 tablespoons softly whipped cream or
    crème fraîche

Preheat oven to 375°F. Beat two eggs with cream and vanilla; set aside. Combine flour, baking powder and salt in medium bowl. Cut in butter with pastry blender or two knives until mixture resembles coarse crumbs. Stir in dates and raisins. Add egg mixture; mix just until dry ingredients are moistened. With floured hands, knead dough four times on lightly floured surface. Place dough on greased cookie sheet; pat into 8-inch circle. With sharp wet knife, gently score dough into six wedges, cutting ¾ of the way into dough. Beat remaining egg with water; brush lightly over dough. Bake 18 to 20 minutes or until golden brown. Cool 5 minutes on wire rack. Cut into wedges. Serve warm with marmalade and whipped cream.

Makes 6 scones

Harvest Mini Chip Muffins

¼ cup (½ stick) butter or margarine
1 cup sugar
1 cup canned pumpkin
2 eggs
2¼ cups all-purpose flour
2 teaspoons baking powder
½ teaspoon baking soda

¾ teaspoon pumpkin pie spice
½ teaspoon salt
½ cup milk
1 cup HERSHEY¿S MINI CHIPS™
    Semi-Sweet Chocolate Chips
½ cup chopped pecans

1. Heat oven to 350°F. Grease or line muffin cups (2½ inches in diameter) with paper bake cups.

2. Beat butter and sugar in large bowl until creamy. Add pumpkin and eggs; blend well. Stir together flour, baking powder, baking soda, pumpkin pie spice and salt; add alternately with milk to pumpkin mixture, beating after each addition just until blended. Stir in small chocolate chips and pecans. Fill muffin cups ⅔ full with batter.

3. Bake 20 to 25 minutes or until wooden pick inserted in center comes out clean. Serve warm.

Makes about 2 dozen muffins

English-Style Scone

Banana Pecan Braid

Dough
- 3 cups bread flour
- ½ cup chopped dates or pitted dates, snipped
- ½ cup chopped pecans, toasted
- ¼ cup sugar
- 2 teaspoons FLEISCHMANN'S® Bread Machine Yeast
- ½ teaspoon salt
- 3 tablespoons butter or margarine, cut up
- 3 tablespoons milk
- 3 tablespoons water (70° to 80°F)
- ½ cup mashed ripe banana
- 1 large egg

Topping
- 1 tablespoon sugar
- ½ teaspoon ground cardamom *or* ¼ teaspoon ground allspice

Add dough ingredients to bread machine pan in the order suggested by manufacturer. Select dough/manual cycle. When cycle is complete, remove dough to floured surface. If necessary, knead in additional flour to make dough easy to handle.

Divide dough into 3 equal pieces; roll each to 15-inch rope. Braid 3 ropes together, pinching ends to seal. Place on greased baking sheet. Cover and let rise in warm, draft-free place until doubled in size, about 1 hour. In small bowl, combine topping ingredients; sprinkle over loaf. Bake at 375°F for 25 to 30 minutes or until done. Remove from baking sheet; cool on wire rack. *Makes 1 loaf*

Note: Dough can be prepared in all size bread machines.

Cranberry Brunch Muffins

- 1 cup chopped fresh cranberries
- ⅓ cup plus ¼ cup sugar, divided
- 2 cups all-purpose flour
- 2 teaspoons baking powder
- ¾ teaspoon salt
- ½ cup butter
- ¾ cup orange juice
- 1 egg, lightly beaten
- 1 teaspoon vanilla
- 2 tablespoons butter, melted

Preheat oven to 400°F. Grease 12-cup muffin pan. Combine cranberries and 1 tablespoon sugar in small bowl. Blend flour, ⅓ cup sugar, baking powder and salt in large bowl. Cut in ½ cup butter until mixture is crumbly. Stir in orange juice, egg and vanilla just until ingredients are moistened. Fold in cranberry mixture; spoon batter into prepared pan.

Bake 20 to 25 minutes or until golden. Cool 5 minutes before removing from pan. Dip tops of muffins in melted butter; sprinkle with remaining 3 tablespoons sugar. Serve warm.

Makes 12 muffins

Banana Pecan Braid

Lots o' Chocolate Bread

⅔ cup packed light brown sugar
½ cup butter, softened
1½ cups miniature semi-sweet chocolate chips, divided
2 eggs
2½ cups all-purpose flour
1½ cups applesauce

1 teaspoon baking soda
1 teaspoon baking powder
½ teaspoon salt
1½ teaspoons vanilla
½ cup chocolate chips
1 tablespoon shortening (do not use butter, margarine, spread or oil)

Preheat oven to 350°F. Grease 5 (5½×3-inch) mini loaf pans. Beat brown sugar and butter in large bowl with electric mixer until creamy. Melt 1 cup miniature chocolate chips; cool slightly and add to sugar mixture with eggs. Add flour, applesauce, baking soda, baking powder, salt and vanilla; beat until well mixed. Stir in remaining ½ cup miniature chocolate chips. Spoon batter into prepared pans; bake 35 to 40 minutes or until center crack is dry to the touch. Cool 10 minutes before removing from pans.

Place ½ cup chocolate chips and shortening in small microwavable bowl. Microwave at HIGH 1 minute; stir. If necessary, microwave at HIGH an additional 15 seconds at a time, stirring after each heating. Drizzle warm loaves with glaze. Cool completely.   *Makes 5 mini loaves*

Super Brown Bread

2 cups warm water (105° to 115°F)
2 packages active dry yeast
1½ cups whole wheat flour
2½ to 3 cups bread flour, divided
½ cup rolled oats

½ cup packed brown sugar
¼ cup wheat germ
¼ cup vegetable oil
¼ cup molasses
2 teaspoons salt

In large bowl, combine water and yeast. Let stand until dissolved, about 5 minutes. Add whole wheat flour, 1 cup bread flour, oats, brown sugar, wheat germ, oil, molasses and salt. Beat until smooth. Add additional bread flour to make soft dough.

Knead 10 minutes or until smooth. Place in greased bowl, turning to grease top; cover and let rise until doubled.

Form into two loaves; place in two 8×4-inch greased loaf pans and let rise until doubled. Bake at 450°F for 10 minutes. *Reduce oven temperature to 325°F; bake 35 minutes.*

Makes 2 loaves (16 slices each)

Favorite recipe from **North Dakota Wheat Commission**

Lots o' Chocolate Bread

Soda Bread

1½ cups whole wheat flour
1 cup all-purpose flour
½ cup rolled oats
¼ cup sugar
1½ teaspoons baking powder
½ teaspoon baking soda
¼ teaspoon ground cinnamon
⅓ cup raisins (optional)
¼ cup walnuts (optional)
1¼ cups low-fat buttermilk
1 tablespoon vegetable oil

Preheat oven to 375°F. Combine whole wheat flour, all-purpose flour, oats, sugar, baking powder, baking soda and cinnamon in large bowl. Stir in raisins and walnuts, if desired. Gradually stir in buttermilk and oil until dough forms. Knead in bowl for 30 seconds. Spray loaf pan with nonstick cooking spray; place dough in pan. Bake 40 to 50 minutes or until wooden toothpick inserted in center comes out clean.   *Makes 16 slices*

Favorite recipe from **The Sugar Association, Inc.**

Peach Streusel Coffee Cake

Streusel
½ cup QUAKER® Oats (quick or old fashioned, uncooked)
⅓ cup sugar
3 tablespoons margarine, melted
½ teaspoon ground cinnamon
⅛ teaspoon ground nutmeg (optional)

Coffee Cake
1 cup sugar
½ cup (1 stick) margarine, softened
1½ teaspoons vanilla
4 egg whites
1½ cups all-purpose flour
¾ cup QUAKER® Oats (quick or old fashioned, uncooked)
1 tablespoon baking powder
½ teaspoon baking soda
¾ cup light sour cream
1 (16-ounce) can sliced peaches, drained
or 1 cup sliced fresh peaches

Heat oven to 350°F. Spray 9-inch square baking pan with no-stick cooking spray or grease lightly. For streusel, combine all ingredients; mix well. Set aside. For coffee cake, beat sugar, margarine and vanilla until fluffy. Add egg whites; mix until smooth. Combine flour, oats, baking powder and baking soda; mix well. Add to sugar mixture alternately with sour cream, beginning and ending with dry ingredients; mix well after each addition. Spread into prepared pan. Pat canned peach slices dry with paper towels; arrange over batter. Sprinkle with streusel. Bake 50 to 55 minutes or until wooden pick inserted in center comes out clean. Serve warm.   *Makes 16 servings*

Soda Bread

Corn Bread

1 cup all-purpose flour	**½ teaspoon salt**
1 cup yellow cornmeal	**1 cup milk**
⅓ cup sugar	**⅓ cup vegetable oil**
2 teaspoons baking powder	**1 egg**

1. Preheat oven to 400°F. Grease 8-inch square baking pan.

2. Combine flour, cornmeal, sugar, baking powder and salt in large bowl; set aside. Combine milk, oil and egg in small bowl until blended. Stir milk mixture into flour mixture just until moistened. Spread batter evenly into prepared pan.

3. Bake 20 to 25 minutes or until golden brown and toothpick inserted in center comes out clean. Cut into squares. Serve warm. *Makes 9 servings*

Corn Muffins: Preheat oven to 400°F. Prepare batter as directed in steps 1 and 2, except spoon batter into 12 (2½-inch) greased or paper-lined muffin cups. Bake 20 minutes or until golden brown and toothpick inserted in center comes out clean. Immediately remove from pan; cool on wire rack 10 minutes. Serve warm. Makes 12 muffins.

Double Apple Bran Cereal Muffins

1¼ cups flour	**1 egg**
1 tablespoon CALUMET® Baking Powder	**½ cup applesauce**
¼ teaspoon ground cinnamon	**1 small apple, peeled, cored and finely**
¼ teaspoon salt	**chopped (1 cup)**
2 cups POST® Bran Flakes Cereal	**⅓ cup firmly packed brown sugar**
1 cup fat free milk	**2 tablespoons margarine, melted**

HEAT oven to 400°F. Spray 12-cup muffin pan with no stick cooking spray.

MIX flour, baking powder, cinnamon and salt in large bowl. Mix cereal and milk in another bowl; let stand 3 minutes.

BEAT egg in small bowl; stir in applesauce, chopped apple, sugar and margarine. Stir into cereal mixture. Add to flour mixture; stir just until moistened. (Batter will be lumpy.) Spoon batter into prepared muffin pan, filling each cup ⅔ full.

BAKE 20 minutes or until golden brown. Serve warm. *Makes 12 muffins*

Challah

1-Pound Loaf
½ cup water
1 large egg
2 tablespoons margarine, cut up
1 teaspoon salt
2 cups bread flour
4 teaspoons sugar
1½ teaspoons FLEISCHMANN'S® Bread
    Machine Yeast
1 yolk of large egg
1 tablespoon water

1½-Pound Loaf
¾ cup water
1 large egg
3 tablespoons margarine, cut up
1¼ teaspoons salt
3 cups bread flour
2 tablespoons sugar
2 teaspoons FLEISCHMANN'S® Bread
    Machine Yeast
1 yolk of large egg
1 tablespoon water

Add water, egg, margarine, salt, bread flour, sugar and yeast to bread machine pan in the order suggested by manufacturer. Select dough/manual cycle. When cycle is complete, remove dough from machine to lightly floured surface. If necessary, knead in enough additional flour to make dough easy to handle. (For 1½-pound recipe, divide dough in half to make 2 loaves.)

For each loaf, divide dough into 2 pieces, one about ⅔ of the dough and the other about ⅓ of the dough. Divide larger piece into 3 equal pieces; roll into 12-inch ropes. Place ropes on greased baking sheet. Braid by bringing left rope under center rope; lay it down. Bring right rope under new center rope; lay it down. Repeat to end. Pinch ends to seal. Divide remaining piece into 3 equal pieces. Roll into 10-inch ropes; braid. Place small braid on top of large braid. Pinch ends firmly to seal and to secure to large braid. Cover and let rise in warm, draft-free place until almost doubled in size, 15 to 20 minutes. Lightly beat egg yolk and 1 tablespoon water; brush over braids.

Bake at 375°F for 25 to 30 minutes or until done, covering with foil after 15 minutes to prevent excess browning. (For even browning when baking two loaves, switch positions of baking sheets halfway through baking.) Remove from baking sheets; cool on wire racks. *Makes 1 or 2 loaves*

❦ *Hearty Soups* ❦

Chicken Tortilla Soup

1 clove garlic, minced
1 can (14½ ounces) chicken broth
1 jar (16 ounces) mild chunky-style salsa
2 tablespoons *Frank's® RedHot®* Cayenne
    Pepper Sauce
1 package (10 ounces) fully cooked carved
    chicken breasts

1 can (8¾ ounces) whole kernel corn,
    undrained
1 tablespoon chopped fresh cilantro
    (optional)
1 cup crushed tortilla chips
½ cup (2 ounces) shredded Monterey Jack
    cheese

1. Heat *1 teaspoon oil* in large saucepan over medium-high heat. Cook garlic 1 minute or until tender. Add broth, *¾ cup water,* salsa and *Frank's RedHot* Sauce. Stir in chicken, corn and cilantro. Heat to boiling. Reduce heat to medium-low. Cook, covered, 5 minutes.

2. Stir in tortillas and cheese. Serve hot.   *Makes 4 servings*

Prep Time: 5 minutes
Cook Time: 6 minutes

Chicken Tortilla Soup

Veg•All® Italian Soup

2 tablespoons butter
1 cup diced onion
1 cup shredded cabbage
2 cups water
2 cans (14½ ounces each) stewed tomatoes
1 can (15 ounces) VEG•ALL® Original
    Mixed Vegetables, drained

1 tablespoon chopped fresh parsley
½ teaspoon dried basil
½ teaspoon dried oregano
½ teaspoon black pepper

In large saucepan, melt butter. Stir in onion and cabbage. Heat for 2 minutes. Add water; cover and simmer for 10 minutes. Stir in tomatoes, Veg•All, and seasonings. Simmer for 10 minutes.

Makes 6 servings

Mama Mia Minestrone Magnifico

2 tablespoons extra-virgin olive oil
8 ounces crimini mushrooms, cut into
    ½-inch pieces (3 cups)
1 yellow summer squash (6 ounces), cut
    into ½-inch cubes (1¼ cups)
½ small eggplant, cut into ½-inch cubes
    (1 cup)
4 ounces green beans, cut diagonally into
    ½-inch pieces (1 cup)
6 cups water
1 (26-ounce) jar NEWMAN'S OWN®
    Roasted Garlic and Peppers Sauce

1 cup Burgundy wine
1 cup uncooked orzo pasta
1 (15½- to 19-ounce) can white kidney
    beans (cannellini), drained
4 medium tomatoes (1 pound), chopped
    (2 cups)
4 fresh basil leaves, chopped
1 tablespoon chopped fresh Italian parsley
¾ cup freshly grated Parmesan cheese
½ cup pine nuts, toasted

In 12-inch nonstick skillet, heat oil; sauté mushrooms, squash, eggplant and green beans over medium-high heat 10 minutes, stirring constantly, until golden and tender.

Combine water, pasta sauce and wine in 6-quart saucepot and bring to a boil. Add orzo and simmer 10 minutes, stirring occasionally.

Add sautéed vegetables, white beans, chopped tomatoes, basil and parsley; simmer 5 minutes, stirring occasionally.

Serve with Parmesan cheese and pine nuts to sprinkle on top.

Makes 8 servings

Veg•All® Italian Soup

Ranch Clam Chowder

¼ cup chopped onion
3 tablespoons butter or margarine
½ pound fresh mushrooms, sliced
2 tablespoons Worcestershire sauce
1½ cups half-and-half
1 can (10¾ ounces) cream of potato soup
¼ cup dry white wine

1 package (1 ounce) HIDDEN VALLEY®
The Original Ranch® Salad Dressing
& Seasoning Mix
1 can (10 ounces) whole baby clams,
undrained
Chopped parsley

In 3-quart saucepan, cook onion in butter over medium heat until onion is soft but not browned. Add mushrooms and Worcestershire sauce. Cook until mushrooms are soft and pan juices have almost evaporated. In medium bowl, whisk together half-and-half, potato soup, wine and salad dressing mix until smooth. Drain clam liquid into dressing mixture; stir into mushrooms in pan. Cook, uncovered, until soup is heated through but not boiling. Add clams to soup; cook until heated through. Garnish each serving with parsley.

Makes 6 servings

Butternut Squash Soup

2 tablespoons butter or margarine
1 medium onion, chopped
2 cloves garlic, minced
3 medium carrots, diced
2 stalks celery, diced
1 butternut squash, peeled, seeded and
diced

1 medium potato, peeled and diced
3 cans (14½ ounces each) ready-to-serve
chicken broth
½ cup honey
½ teaspoon dried thyme leaves, crushed
Salt and pepper, to taste

In large pot, melt butter over medium heat. Stir in onion and garlic. Cook and stir until lightly browned, about 5 minutes. Stir in carrots and celery. Cook and stir until tender, about 5 minutes. Stir in squash, potato, chicken broth, honey and thyme. Bring mixture to a boil; reduce heat and simmer 30 to 45 minutes, or until vegetables are tender. Remove from heat and cool slightly. Working in small batches, transfer mixture to blender or food processor; process until smooth. Return puréed soup to pot. Season to taste with salt and pepper. Heat until hot and serve.

Makes 6 servings

Favorite recipe from **National Honey Board**